TIPS FOR YOUR JOURNEY

- Be gentle and patient with yourself

When you work on improving your skills, you must be patient and give yourself time to observe the changes. It might take you several months to witness a lasting change.

- Simply try to improve. Perfection does not exist.

As a human being, accept that you will make mistakes. What is important is to learn from those mistakes. When you are on the way to develop EQ skills, it is essential to chase success, not perfection. Don't be too hard on yourself. This will only result in amplifying the problem. Take your time and catch yourself when emotions take over.

- Simply focus on the here and now

Every time a situation presents itself, you might have a different reaction to it. Even if you plan on not messing up, your actions can prove to be quite different. Treat every emotion as its own and separate. Every situation you face requires making sure that you deal with it bravely.

- Stop judging yourself and focus on facts

Thoughts have the power to make or break your mental state of mind. Therefore, your thoughts and emotions should not cross a limit wherein you feel there is no room for improvement. Instead of demotivating yourself, replace your thoughts with positive ones. Factual statements or thoughts allow space for improvement.

- Recognize that you are the only one in charge of your actions

Negativity and blame games often feed on each other. If you wish to improve yourself, you should take complete responsibility for your actions. If you blame yourself all the time, you should know that it is wrong to carry someone else's burden. However, it is wise to accept when you are at fault. If you tend to blame others, it's time to reflect on your responsibilities.

- Feelings are never good or bad, they simply are

There are no good or bad emotions. There are only good or bad reactions to situations. If you aim to improve your emotional intelligence, the first thing to do is stop labeling your emotions. For instance, you may classify guilt as a bad emotion and excitement as a good one. When you attach a specific label to your emotions, you do not allow yourself to understand it completely. On the other hand, when you spend time with an emotion, you become aware of what is causing it. The next time you feel a flood of emotions, take your time to understand why you feel the way you do.

- If you don't feel inspired, simply wait after a good night's sleep

The two best pieces of advice that you can get are to give things time and have patience. Though it is easier said than done, these two tips can help change the course of your life for the better. In certain situations, you may feel the need to jump the gun and make a decision for your internal peace of mind. However, giving things time helps you gain better clarity of situations. It can help you move forward in a better direction and allows you to be in control of your emotions. You look at events from a different perspective. Furthermore, with patience and time, certain situations tend to transform right in front of our eyes. Though waiting may seem uncomfortable, it is wise to try it.

Introduction

Inspiration and motivation are overrated! Yes, for a while, they leave you feeling thrilled and bursting with energy. However, their instability and unpredictability will make it difficult for you to achieve success. We all want to improve our lives and realize our dreams. But the question is how? There are so many steps you can take to improve your life. Perhaps one of the most important steps is to stop your emotions from taking control of your life. You do that by paying attention to them, to the way you react to them, and to how they affect your abilities to make decisions. Focus on improving your emotional intelligence.

Success is not easy. If it were easy, we would all be living our ideal lives. Although developing technical skills is tough, dealing with emotions is way more challenging! Being constantly emotionally attached to everything that you do is draining! The same is true for the incessant roller-coaster of emotions. One day you feel ecstatic like it is the best day of your life, and the next one you just want to give everything up and cry yourself to sleep. Then something happens that leaves you overjoyed. Rinse and repeat. This exhausting cycle serves only to remind you that you are an emotional human being.

Each emotion can also become very intense and feel overwhelming, be it love, fear, hate, or anger. When someone has an emotional personality, this person becomes their emotions. When the person feels anger, all their being transforms into anger. When the person feels love, every inch of their body becomes love. That person loses their rationality, and their decisions and actions will be blinded by the overwhelming emotions they are experiencing at that very moment. Be it fear, anger, love, or another emotion, just like alcohol, emotions can blind you.

By nature, we are emotional creatures. Emotions are constant, whether they are intense or not, and it is easy to forget about our emotional reactions. Experiences will always be emotional at first before you interpret them. Although you have no control of your emotions, your reactions can be controlled. How? By developing good emotional awareness. Emotions can help or hurt you and understanding them will make all the difference in the outcome.

But how do emotions work? When we experience something, a signal is sent to the brain for interpretation. While your emotions pass from the back of your brain, your ability to analyze and think critically rests in the front, logical part of your brain. Information traveling from the back to the front part of your brain goes through the Limbic System. This is where the information is interpreted. To rationalize your actions and decision, the signal must make it to the front of your brain. If you make a decision and take action while an emotion is still processing in the Limbic System, the signal does not make its way to the front, logical part of the brain. Emotional intelligence stems from good communication between the back and front parts of your brain. Hence, for emotional information to be interpreted rationally, you need to have a good level of emotional intelligence. Developing emotional intelligence skills through practice allows for a smooth traveling of information between the two parts of your brain.

While some experiences make it easy for you to be emotionally aware, others do not. A trigger event is an experience that causes you to have a sustained emotional reaction. Your reaction to triggers is uniquely shaped by your past experiences, for instance, childhood memories. If, for example, you remember being constantly yelled at by your mother, then as an adult, perhaps being yelled at by someone will trigger a powerful, poignant emotion. Developing your emotional intelligence will help you spot triggers and deal with them more effectively.

No matter your goals in life, the way you understand and deal with your emotions will make all the difference in your success. Knowledge is great, but action is what counts. This journal will help you to increase your understanding of emotional intelligence and guide you to the life that you desire. You will have an opportunity to reflect on how you are currently dealing with your emotions and practice strategies aimed at improving your emotional intelligence in the long run. After going through this journal, you may well realize that your aspirations are achieved much more easily!

What is emotional intelligence?

Emotional intelligence is the ability to manage your emotions in a positive way to communicate effectively and overcome challenges. If you want to build stronger and healthier relationships, you must develop this aspect of your intelligence. It helps you to such an extent that it can play a pivotal role in achieving your dreams. Furthermore, emotional intelligence helps you better connect with yourself and make wise decisions in life.

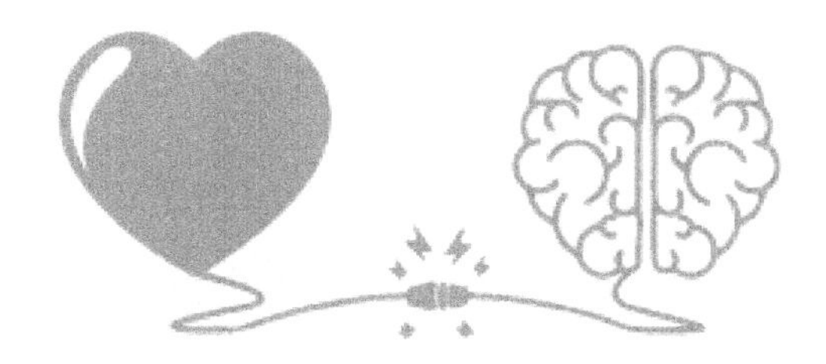

You must have heard of IQ, but do you know what EQ is?

Just like IQ measures your intelligence, EQ (Emotional Quotient) measures your emotional intelligence. It is defined as the ability to access, evaluate, and understand emotions or feelings. Emotional intelligence mainly focuses on factors like identifying and understanding emotions, analyzing how others feel, and having control over one's reactions. Furthermore, it is directed at understanding others' emotions and using the right emotions to boost communication. Finally, it also requires you to relate to others and consider their viewpoint or perspective.

IQ and EQ are often mistaken for one another. However, both these terms are quite different from one another. While EQ is called 'Emotional Quotient,' IQ is known as 'Intelligence Quotient.' Intelligence Quotient is the measure of an individual's intelligence. EQ is characterized as the ability to understand and recognize emotions effectively. Superior performers and leaders are known to have high emotional intelligence.

Similarly, an intelligence quotient is a number that is used to express an individual's intelligence. A person who has a score above 145 is known to be a genius. About two-thirds of the population in the world have an IQ score between 85-115. IQ or intelligence quotient can change over time if an individual wish to learn new ideas or concepts.

Why should you care about emotional intelligence?

Being academically smart is not a sure-shot sign of achieving success. To achieve success, you need to have a combination of skills. Being smart in school but unable to communicate with people will not make you a success! Several other elements play a major role in defining success. Your intelligence will help you land a spot in your choice of college. However, your emotional intelligence will help you manage your emotions and stress during the course. Both intelligence and emotional intelligence are essential for success. Emotional intelligence can help you lead a happy and fulfilled life. You gain better control of your emotions and understand other people too. In the modern world, there is a lot of emphasis on emotional intelligence everywhere. It not only helps you connect better with yourself but others as well. When you are finely tuned with your emotions, you learn to handle them better.

The different areas in which emotional intelligence plays an important part.

1| Health

If you cannot handle or manage your emotions, you will not be able to deal with stress either. This could lead to several health issues that can turn dangerous. High stress can lead to a rise in blood pressure. Furthermore, it can weaken your immune system or causes issues related to infertility. You are also prone to getting heart attacks or strokes as well. The most crucial step to improve emotional intelligence is to learn to deal with stress and handle emotions in a better way.

2| Performance:

Having good emotional intelligence can help you navigate your life well, motivate others, and excel. Emotional intelligence is now a determining factor that decides whether you can sustain a good relationship with others or not. It is rated as an important aspect and ability. In every aspect of life, you can perform tremendously well if you have a knowledge and understanding of EQ under your belt.

3| Mental health

Uncontrolled stress and emotions are known to impact mental health in negative ways. It could lead to serious depression and anxiety, which can make you feel vulnerable. If you are not able to understand others, handle stress or emotions, or get comfortable with situations, it can get difficult for you to form healthy relationships. This can leave you feeling lonely, which can affect your mental health.

4| Relationships

When you understand your own emotions and learn how to control them, you can better convey your feelings. You are also better able to understand others' emotions. This allows you to form stronger, deeper relationships.

How does emotional intelligence help you improve your life?

Emotional Intelligence is known to have a meaningful role in succeeding in life. Studies also report that EQ has a significant role in physical and mental health. A survey conducted revealed that people with higher emotional intelligence perform better than people with lower emotional intelligence. The ability to understand and sympathize with others' feelings and emotions is key to understanding yourself. How do we achieve success if we do not know our true feelings or emotions? That would be quite hard to decipher. Emotional Intelligence helps you deal with stress, motivates others, improves relationships, and boosts your decision-making skills.

Emotional intelligence is very crucial to handle stressful situations that life throws at you. People who have higher emotional intelligence are known to be better leaders, have good decision-making skills, are calm and composed, resolve conflicts, show empathy, and work on themselves for improvement.

Can emotional intelligence be improved?

Emotional intelligence continues to be one of the most popular skills in the twenty-first century. Its importance has gained a lot of momentum. The truth is that strong EQ is an asset that everyone cherishes on a subconscious level. High levels of emotional intelligence are also known to deliver higher productivity and sales. The best part around this is that EQ can be developed over time. While some people have emotional intelligence as a natural skill, everyone can improve it with practice. It is an indispensable skill that you should develop to give a boost to your success in every activity you undertake.

However, multiple factors play a role in developing emotional intelligence. For example, personality, attitude, and upbringing are important factors determining the level of emotional intelligence in a person.

The five categories of emotional intelligence

1 | Self-regulation:

There is very little control over how or when you experience emotions. However, you can decide how long you want emotion to last within you. Multiple techniques are available, like meditation or yoga, to reduce stress or control anger. These techniques help you look at the bright side of things. Another way you can control emotions is by taking a walk or distracting yourself. Self-regulation consists of having self-control and maintaining your integrity and honesty. Furthermore, it also includes being responsible for your actions and being adaptable.

Finally, it requires you to be open to new thoughts and ideas.

How much control do you think you have over your emotions?

What is your favorite technique to reduce stress or control your emotions?

Are you open to new thoughts and ideas?

If yes, how open do you think you are? If no, write down why.

2| Self-Awareness:

Your ability to understand an emotion when it surfaces plays a significant role in emotional intelligence. Self-awareness is when you start to understand yourself better. If you are aware of your emotions, you can act on them.

There are two major elements of self-awareness. The first one is emotional awareness, which means your ability to understand your feelings and emotions. The second one is self-confidence that involves knowing your capabilities and self-worth.

Are you experiencing any particular emotion right now? If yes, write it down.

What is your best quality?

What motivates you to keep going when things are not going the way you want them to?

3| Empathy

Empathy is defined as the ability to understand how other people feel. It can play a significant role in your life. The more you recognize people's emotions and feelings, the better you can reciprocate towards them. Someone who empathetic understands and accepts others' needs. This person senses what other people need to improve. This creates opportunities to interact with diverse cultures. An empathetic person understands other people well and is respectful of their emotions.

Do you feel sad when any of your friends are going through a difficult time?

What do you do when someone is crying in front of you?

Do you feel happy when you help someone or do charitable work? Share any such experience that you had.

4| Motivation

A positive attitude and precise goals are necessary to motivate yourself for success. Though it is common to lose motivation or let negative thoughts come in, it is up to you to change them to positive thoughts. Look at the bright side of things to help you with motivation. Motivation requires consistent patience to excel. You need to have the right commitment to achieve your goals. Besides, you need to take the initiative to make the best use of opportunities. Lastly, you need to have an optimistic outlook that will not accept defeat come what may.

Set a clear goal that you would like to achieve in a week. Write it down here.

Do you reward yourself when you complete your tasks? Why or why not?

Write any one way in which you will reward yourself when you complete the goal written above.

5| Social Skills

Interpersonal skills play a big role in your success and overall life. In today's modern world, information is just a tap away. Hence, "people skills" have more importance than any other skill. A high level of emotional intelligence is required to understand, recognize, and negotiate with people around you. Some of the most useful social skills are communication, leadership, building bonds, conflict management, cooperation, collaboration, problem-solving, and team-building capabilities.

Do you find it easy or difficult to talk to new people? Why or why not?

How do you resolve conflicts with your friends?

Do you like to participate in group activities? Why or why not?

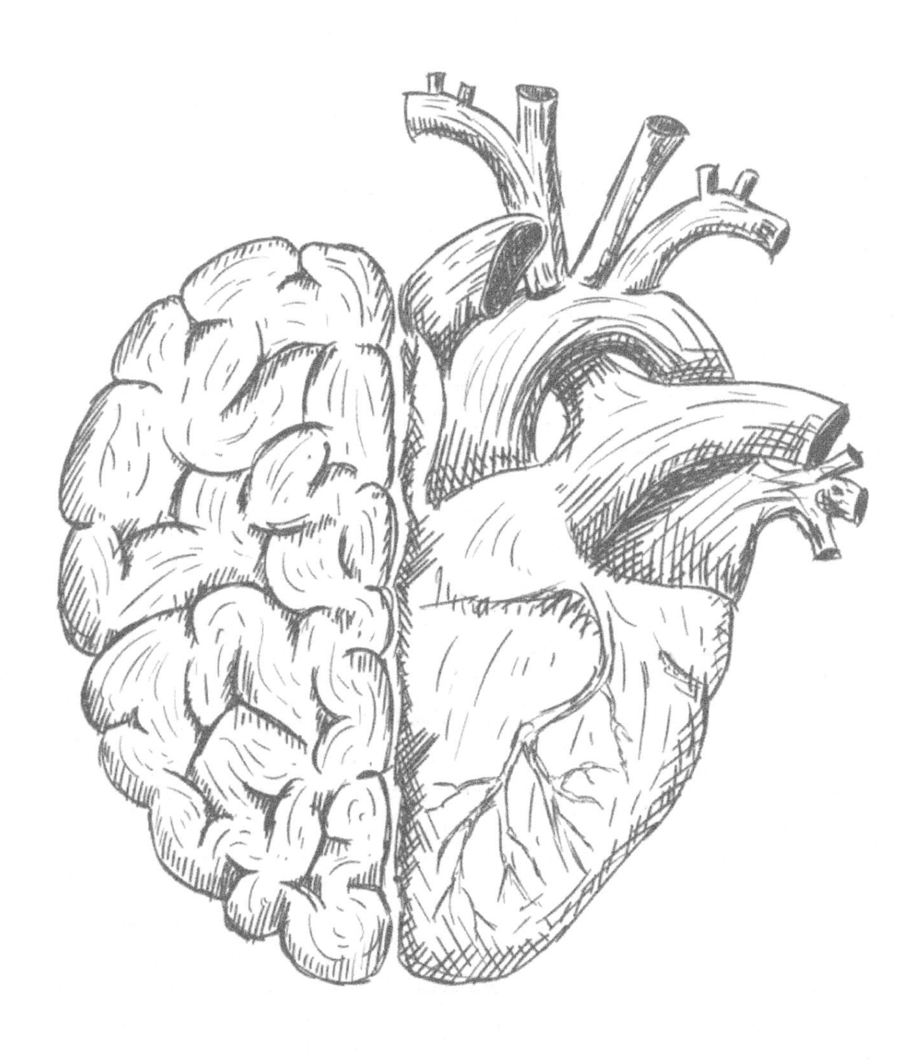

How can you develop a good EQ?

1| Know your feelings

The first thing to building emotional intelligence is to know how you feel. It is important to be aware of your feelings and emotions. Your true feelings might leave you in wonder, or you may recognize that you are quite sad, lonely, or depressed. You might also be going through anxiety or stress issues. However, be sure not to judge your emotions at all. Be yourself and observe how you feel about yourself. Just remember not to be too hard or harsh on yourself. Be it any emotion you feel, make sure that you are aware of it. This way, you can carry on with the next step, which is to channel your emotions.

In the past week, would you say that you were relatively happy or sad? Write down any one reason for it.

Remember a time you felt angry when someone shouted at you. How do you think someone else might feel if you get angry at them?

Mention one instance when you communicated your problems to a friend. How did that make you feel?

2| Channel emotions

Always being on the lookout to control your emotions is a bad idea. You must accept the fact that you do not have any control over your feelings or emotions. It is a part of the natural process of your body and mind. However, what you can do is channel your emotions or distract yourself. You cannot run away from a feeling, but you can react to it. There are no good or bad emotions, but only good or bad reactions to the emotions you feel. For example, anger can be an emotion wherein you end up hurting others or yourselves. However, if you choose to turn over the emotion into something good, you can develop emotional intelligence. Similarly, joy is a happy emotion. However, it can be bad if you receive it by harming or destroying others.

What do you do when you have a problem that you feel you cannot discuss with anyone?

Do you practice breathing exercises? If not, would you like to try? If yes, what are your reasons?

Do you usually practice journal writing? If yes, how does journaling improve your life?

3| Stay Motivated

To develop emotional intelligence, it is important that you stay motivated. Some people look for motivation to start something new, and then within a few weeks, the motivation is lost. The best way to approach it would be to first start the activity and then look for motivation to achieve the desired task. For instance, if writing is something you want to do, start with a small outline first. Then think of the next step. Planning each step one by one will give you the desired motivation required for the task. Once you know your emotions well, you can use them in the right way.

Mention any one person who motivates you when you feel lost. What does this person do to motivate you?

Who is your role model in life and why?

Tonight, plan what activities you want to do tomorrow. Write “done” here when you complete them.

4| Recognize emotions in others

Just as you would recognize emotions in yourself, you need to know the emotions of others too. This will lead to healthier and stronger relationships. Any relationship starts with being respectful of one another's emotions. You can do it only by empathizing and being considerate with others. It requires you to listen to your feelings and emotional needs and to be honest with others regarding these feelings. When you empathize with someone, it does not mean that you understand them completely. It just means that you accept them for who they are and respect that. You need to value their existence and appreciate them as they are. This way, you can form healthy relationships and a strong bond with people.

How well do you think you can identify other people's emotions?

Do you listen when someone wants to share a problem with you?

Do you feel the need to change people around you?

5 | Learn to manage stress

Each one of us faces moments of stress in our lives. However, the important thing here is how we handle stress. How we respond to stressful situations determines our emotional intelligence. To build our EQ, we need to learn how to deal with stress and anxiety. It is also crucial to learn how to stay calm in such situations. When you feel the most pressure, it is important to be calm and composed. Try to look at the bright side of things, however hard it may seem. There are several ways to handle stress, including taking a walk, meditating, having a hobby, and practicing yoga.

Mention a stressful situation you encountered in life. How did you overcome it?

Do you practice yoga or meditation? If not, would you like to try?

What is your favorite hobby and why did you choose this particular one?

6| Practice empathy

Empathy is looking at the world from a different perspective. It is an essential aspect of mental health. The first step to building empathy is to begin at home. Small acts of kindness can go a long way in building your emotional intelligence. A simple thank you note, having a heart-to-heart conversation, or offering help to a needy person is all it takes to get started. You could listen to a friend undergoing hardships and help them out, or you could offer help to people who need it. This act builds your relationship with people and increases their trust in you.

Mention the last time you said thank you to any of your family members.

Do you feel more connected to someone who listens to your hardships? Why?

Give a compliment to someone today. Write down how their reaction makes you feel.

The most common emotional triggers

1| Fear

Fear is quite a powerful emotion that can overtake your thoughts or feelings. It is widely used as a marketing tool to boost sales for a product. This makes consumers loyal to a particular brand, service, or sales. Fear is an emotion that can be used to manipulate people and their thought processes. Though it is not the best-recommended option, it is used in a tactical form in marketing. Similarly, fear can be quite a disturbing emotion and has tremendous power to change you.

Write down any one thing that you are afraid of. How do you choose to overcome this fear?

Do you think fear has ever affected your quality of life? If yes, how?

Is there any instance when you did something out of your comfort zone? If yes, mention how it made you feel.

2| Belongingness

Every human being has a strong desire to belong to someone. It can either be a family, a group, a clan, or a social network. Sometimes, even though the activity may be wrong, the desire to feel accepted remains. The need to belong somewhere is quite strong in humans and has the power to trigger emotions. For example, football fans excitedly gather to support their team.

Are you a part of any club or a group? If not, would you like to join one? Why or why not?

How connected do you feel to your family?

Mention the last time you celebrated something with your loved ones.

3 | Guilt

Guilt is another powerful and very prevalent emotion. If you happen to commit any mistake, the first emotion that engulfs your mind is guilt. However, it can be used as an advantage or a disadvantage. As recommended earlier, take responsibility for your actions, but do not blame others for mistakes or faults. If you are the one who is at fault, it is okay to feel guilty for your actions. On the other hand, if you are not the one at fault, you need not feel guilty.

Do you feel bad when you make a mistake? How hard do you find it to accept making a mistake?

Would you confess if you saw someone else being punished for something that you did?

Is there anything in your life that makes you feel guilty? If yes, how do you plan to forgive yourself?

4| Trust

Relationships need trust. Without trust, you cannot form any strong and healthy relationship. Hence, trust is the foundation of any relationship. If this trust is broken, it has the power or strength to break your relationship completely. Just as any other emotion, trust has its advantages and disadvantages.

How easily do you trust people around you?

Who do you generally confide in? Why do you trust this person so much?

Have you tried trust-building exercises with your significant other? If no, would you like to try someday?

Be aware of your trigger points

Sometimes, you might feel that you have reached the limit of your patience when something irritates you. For instance, if a person in the room is too loud, you might feel worked up. If they constantly seek attention, this can irk you, especially if you are the calm and composed type. For instance, you would hate drama queens who are just full of themselves. You are the kind who prefers to get straight to the point and avoid unnecessary acting.

Such a person is sure to flip your switch and make you frustrated. You might not be the one to be blunt or outspoken. However, your body language can make your pretense quite evident. Hence, it is crucial to understand what pushes your buttons. This will help you understand your emotions and handle such situations well. You can then stay calm when such a situation arises. First and foremost, you need to identify particular people and situations that trigger your emotions.

Many people and situations can trigger your buttons. Having a good understanding of such people and situations will make the process less complicated. Moreover, it will not be a big surprise for you. For starters, begin by writing down your trigger points. Being aware of these buttons is essential for maintaining a good temperament.

What is one thing that irritates you the most?

How do you generally react to an irksome person or event?

Have you tried the counting technique when you feel angry? If not, would you like to try it out the next time you are furious?

Practices to train yourself to tolerate emotions

Though it might not be at a conscious level, your mind and heart can sway in two different directions. While you may want to choose an emotional way, your mind may force you to go the rational way. This tug of war can be a huge issue. If you face such a situation, it is best to write down a list of the arguments on both ends. Be clear, honest, and truthful when you jot down the list. This list will allow you to make a better decision and help you see situations in a better light. You can also witness the importance of your emotions and better manage them.

While the heart thinks emotionally, the mind is always rational. The whole point of writing down the list is to understand each side's pros and cons before choosing one. While your emotional side may not think practically, your rational side may not support your emotional way of thinking. Hence the. Ask yourself questions and be transparent with your decisions. While your feelings are always there with or without acknowledgment, they should not come in the way of rational thinking. The next time you have a stressful situation, write down your list. Take your time to organize your thoughts and feelings before you write the list. Once your list is ready, you can have a close look at which side of the argument deserves a say in your decision. You can then make a wise decision.

Breathing: During stressful moments, you can simply focus or concentrate on breathing. This simple technique is quite powerful to help you relax. It is known to calm your nerves and distract you from stress or anxiety. You can also try different techniques, like taking a walk or spending quality time in nature. There are several different things you can do to tolerate your emotions.

Relaxing: The next simple thing you can do during a tense moment is just to relax. Though it may sound quite absurd, relaxing will ease your tensions. It will help you calm down and distract your mind from the moment. You could either engage in some of your favorite hobbies or do something that you love doing.

Staying Still: You can just stay still while you face such moments of despair. Give your body and mind time to reflect on the events. This will clear all your doubts and queries. As mentioned earlier, being patient is one of the best ways to tackle a challenging situation.

What is self-talk and why is it important?

Individuals have multiple thoughts going around their minds in a single day. As these thoughts are processed in their mind, chemicals are produced in the brain. These chemicals are known to trigger several reactions in the body. Did you know that there is a strong link between how you feel and what you think? Your body and mind are connected. At times, you do not even realize how much time you waste thinking about unnecessary stuff.

It is practically impossible to keep track of every emotion that you go through. You cannot focus on every emotion and think about whether it is a positive or negative influence. However, some peculiar thoughts have the most impact on you. These thoughts force you to talk to yourself. Though you may not recognize when you have these thoughts, it happens daily. Each one of us has an internal voice that we speak to. We might congratulate ourselves or instruct ourselves to remain calm.

We tend to communicate with our thoughts, which is called "self-talk." It is quite important to control this self-talk. Once you start getting better at it, you will better recognize and manage your emotions. Furthermore, you will be able to focus on the right things and better handle situations. Regularly engaging in positive self-talk will help you throughout the day. Hence, make sure you keep negative self-talk at bay.

Have you ever faced any situation where your mind suggested one thing while your heart said something else? If yes, write it down.

When you face a stressful situation, do you make a pros and cons list to help you choose your actions? If yes, how does this help you? If not, would you like to try?

Try to take deep breaths the next time you feel stressed or anxious. If you find that this helps you, write "better" here.

Observe the ripple effect from your emotions

Have you ever wondered why we spend so much of our time thinking? How do emotions have such a big impact on our lives? Why do we behave or act in a certain way? Our emotions influence our lives and how we react to situations. However, two factors play a significant role in deciding how we manage our emotions. The first is our attitude or personality, and the second is our upbringing.

The ripple effect is a situation which not only affects you but also the people around you. Just as you throw a stone in the river, you might notice ripples being generated. This one stone produces multiple other ripples. As a parallel, when you feel an emotion, it can affect others around you. You can observe the after-effects of a ripple effect on how it impacts other people.

To gain explicit knowledge and understanding of the ripple effect, you first need to watch your behavior.

Recognize and be aware of your emotions to understand how it affects others. You can also ask other people to realize how your emotions affect them. Once you know the effect of your emotions and their impact on others, you will learn to choose the ripples wisely.

Do you recall any time when your emotions caused an effect on someone around you? If yes, write it down.

Would you say that you have an optimistic personality or a pessimistic one?

How do you think your personality affects the way you react to situations?

Lean into your discomfort. It's not as difficult as it sounds!

The negative side to increasing your self-awareness is the reality of discovering who you are. Once you try to be self-aware, you start looking at yourself in a different light. While some events may shock you, others can be expected. If you need to improve yourself, you need to come to terms with your reality. Avoiding problems will not solve anything. If you ignore what you need to change, you will not learn the art of self-awareness. Emotions cannot be avoided. Hence, it is best to move forward with the emotion, know what is causing it, and overcome it.

This applies to any emotion, be it anger, boredom, confusion, or turmoil. However small it may be, ignoring an emotion prevents you from any opportunity to work on them. Similarly, not giving emotions the attention they deserve will not make them disappear. You will simply experience them at times when you do not see them coming. The best part about being self-aware is an increased focus and ability to concentrate. Furthermore, it gives you a chance to make positive use of your emotions. Leaning into your discomfort offers you a chance to improve yourself.

Mention one thing that you want to change about yourself.

What steps, if any, do you think you can take to cause the above change?

Do you feel better or worse when you suppress your emotions?

Relationships require work, too!

Relationship management is quite an essential component of skills like self-awareness, social awareness, and self-management. It can be defined as the ability to be aware of your emotions as well as other's emotions to have healthy communication. This leads to stronger relationships. Individuals who know the importance of relationships are very aware of maintaining them, even with people they aren't fond of. Strong relationships require years of work. It comprises how you understand others, how you treat them, and how much you value your relationship.

If you have strong connections with people, it is easier to communicate. No two relationships are the same, hence you need to put in different kinds of efforts in each one for it to flourish. You might get along with some people while you may not with others. However, it is entirely dependent on you on how you wish to strengthen the bond. Relationship management is useful in every walk of life. It is okay to have a viewpoint or a strong opinion about someone. However, the relationship still deserves an opportunity to grow. Relationship management skills are crucial for your development and success.

Mention any two different people in your life whose presence you cherish.

What is your relationship with the above two people?

Do you think your bond with these people helps you in your development and success?

What is social awareness and how does it play in your emotional wellbeing?

Social awareness is defined as the ability to understand other people's emotions and realize what they mean. It means to realize and understand their emotions, even if you do not feel the same way. Social awareness requires you to accept others' emotions without any judgment. This skill requires you to focus on and absorb critical information. Two important skills that are part of social awareness: listening and observing, which go hand in hand. To have good social awareness, it is important to listen well and observe the emotions of people around you. Similarly, to listen and observe well, you need to stop multitasking and focus on what is important.

You need to stop overthinking, over-analyzing, or talking too much to gain social awareness. Though you may find it difficult at first to focus on listening, with constant practice, you will be able to accomplish that goal. Social awareness is a necessary skill to master. While listening or observing others, you might observe that you have better ideas. However, it is simply best to avoid talking too much and allow things to take place in their natural form.

Do you engage in other activities while talking to someone? If yes, why?

Do you observe the people around you? Why or why not?

Do you overthink or overanalyze situations? If yes, when are you going to practice controlling this trait?

What is self-management and why is it important?

Self-management, defined as the ability to know your emotions and react accordingly, is heavily dependent on your self-awareness. This ability helps you positively direct your behavior. It also includes being thoughtful about situations and events. Sometimes, your emotions might create turmoil or havoc in your mind. In such situations, self-management is key. Once you accept your emotions, you can come about with the best decision for yourself. One of the biggest obstacles that people face is managing their behavior. When you face such a situation, allow yourself to think first and then react.

This will help you make better decisions and be accountable for your actions. If you are otherwise calm but tend to react in outrageous ways while stressed, developing self-management is a good idea. Trying to be self-aware will make you better realize what you are feeling. Hence, you can better handle your emotions, without causing hurt to yourself or others. Working on your self-management skills will prove helpful in giving an appropriate response in testing times. It will allow you to focus on the right things positively.

How much control do you think you have over your behavior?

Have you ever hurt someone knowingly or unknowingly? If yes, do you think your emotions had a role to play in that situation?

How much time do you generally take to make your decisions in a stressful situation? Why?

How self-awareness will help you achieve your emotional goals

Being self-aware is defined as having a conscious knowledge of your feelings, character, and nature. Self-awareness is a skill that requires you to be completely aware of who you are as a person, be it good or bad. This requires you to come to terms with your attitude, behavior, personality, and desires. When you learn to be self-aware, you might come across interesting shades of yourself. Being self-aware allows you to react better to situations and manage your emotions effectively. You need to be in sync with what is going on in your mind and heart. If you wish to work on being self-aware, you need to concentrate on your feelings, behaviors, reactions, habits, and thoughts.

You ought to be aware of the different aspects that lie within you. While we might have an image of ourselves in mind, being self-aware shows you a different side that you might or might not have known. The whole point of being self-aware is to know your emotions well, learn what is causing them, and look for ways to handle them better. If you have difficulty dealing with anger, for instance, it is best to be aware of your tone and language. This will give you the necessary insight into your behavior and help you change it. Once you recognize your triggers, you can effectively manage and handle them better.

Mention one thing that you greatly desire and indicate why.

Mention three of your strengths and three of your weaknesses.

Do you think your above awareness can play a role in achieving your desire written above?

Made in United States
North Haven, CT
13 March 2023